Plus

Nocturnal Animals

Red Foxes

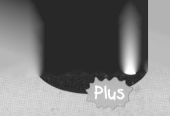

by J. Angelique Johnson

Consulting Editor: Gail Saunders-Smith, PhD

Consultant: Tanya Dewey, PhD
University of Michigan Museum of Zoology

CAPSTONE PRESS
a capstone imprint

Pebble Plus is published by Capstone Press,
1710 Roe Crest Drive, North Mankato, Minnesota 56003.
www.capstonepub.com

Books published by Capstone Press are manufactured with paper
containing at least 10 percent post-consumer waste.

Library of Congress Cataloging-in-Publication Data
Johnson, J. Angelique.
  Red foxes / by J. Angelique Johnson.
     p. cm. — (Pebble plus. Nocturnal animals.)
  Includes bibliographical references and index.
  Summary: "Simple text and full-color photos explain the habitat, life cycle, range, and behavior of red foxes"—
Provided by publisher.
  ISBN 978-1-4296-5285-8 (library binding)
  ISBN 978-1-4296-6195-9 (paperback)
  1. Red fox—Juvenile literature. I. Title.
QL737.C22J637 2011
599.775—dc22   2010028744

Editorial Credits
Katy Kudela, editor; Ashlee Suker, designer; Marcie Spence, media researcher; Laura Manthe, production specialist

Photo Credits
Alamy: First Light, 13, Gay Bumgarner, 7; Ardea: Duncan Usher, 15, John Daniels, cover; iStockphoto: allenlthornton,
9, phototerry, 21; Minden Pictures: Andrew Cooper, 17, Andy Rouse, 19; Shutterstock: Daniel Gale, 11, mlorenz, 1,
Yanik Chauvin, 5

Note to Parents and Teachers

The Nocturnal Animals series supports national science standards related to life science. This
book describes and illustrates red foxes. The images support early readers in understanding
the text. The repetition of words and phrases helps early readers learn new words. This book
also introduces early readers to subject-specific vocabulary words, which are defined in the
Glossary section. Early readers may need assistance to read some words and to use the Table of
Contents, Glossary, Read More, Internet Sites, and Index sections of the book.

Printed in the United States of America in North Mankato, Minnesota.
122011
006506R

Table of Contents

Clever Hunters

Red foxes move in the shadows.

These nocturnal animals

hunt mostly at night.

They look for food

while other animals sleep.

Red foxes creep through forests,
mountains, and grasslands.
They dig holes into hillsides.
They find openings in dead trees.
These homes are called dens.

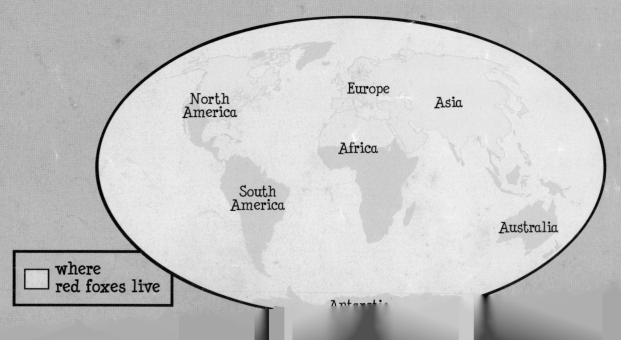

where
red foxes live

North
America

Europe

Asia

Africa

South
America

Australia

Antarcti…

Up Close!

Red foxes have long fur.

Most are reddish-brown.

Others are black or silver.

Adults weigh between 7 and

30 pounds (3 and 14 kilograms).

Red foxes have thick,
bushy tails with white tips.
They wrap their tails
around their bodies to sleep.
Their tails keep them warm.

Finding Food

Red foxes see well in the dark.

But these sneaky hunters

use their ears to listen.

They use their noses

to sniff out prey.

Pounce! Red foxes use
their paws to catch prey.
Red foxes eat mice, birds,
fish, insects, and berries.
They eat anything they can find.

Growing Up

Between winter and spring, females give birth to two to five kits. Kits are born gray. Their fur often changes color in the first month.

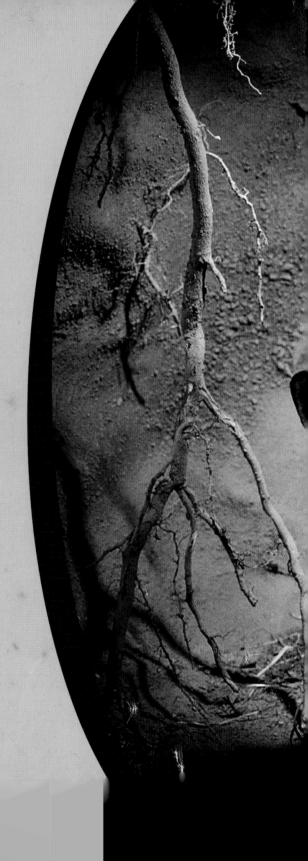

When kits are two months old,

their parents teach them to hunt.

At six months, kits leave the den.

Young foxes find their own homes.

Staying Safe

Predators hunt young red foxes.

Scared foxes show their teeth.

They are quick to run.

Safe foxes live up to

four years in the wild.

Glossary

creep—to move very slowly and quietly

den—a small, protected space where a wild animal lives

hillside—the sloping side of a hill

kit—a young fox

nocturnal—happening at night; a nocturnal animal is active at night

predator—an animal that hunts other animals for food

prey—an animal that is hunted by another animal for food

shadow—a dark shape made when something blocks light

Read More

Doudna, Kelly. *It's a Baby Red Fox!* Baby Mammals. Edina: ABDO, 2008.

Meredith, Susan. *Night Animals.* Beginners Nature. Eveleth, Minn.: Usborne Books, 2007.

Internet Sites

FactHound offers a safe, fun way to find Internet sites related to this book. All of the sites on FactHound have been researched by our staff.

Here's all you do:

Visit *www.facthound.com*

Type in this code: 9781429652858

Check out projects, games and lots more at **www.capstonekids.com**

Index

Word Count: 215

Grade: 1

Early-Intervention Level: 18